DATE DUE

JAN 2 4 2011	
APR 0 1 2011	
MAY 2 6 2011	
JUL 0 7 2011	

DEMCO, INC. 38-2931

LIVE IT:
RESPECT

MOLLY ALOIAN

Crabtree Publishing Company
www.crabtreebooks.com

Crabtree character Sketches

Author: Molly Aloian
Coordinating editor: Bonnie Dobkin
Publishing plan research and development:
  Sean Charlebois, Reagan Miller
  Crabtree Publishing Company
Editor: Reagan Miller
Proofreader: Crystal Sikkens
Editorial director: Kathy Middleton
Production coordinator: Margaret Salter
Prepress technician: Margaret Salter

Logo design: Samantha Crabtree
Project Manager: Santosh Vasudevan (Q2AMEDIA)
Art Direction: Rahul Dhiman (Q2AMEDIA)
Design: Rohit Juneja and Niyati Gosain (Q2AMEDIA)
Illustrations: Q2AMEDIA
Front Cover: Children in Denmark interview their grandparents for
  the Grandparent Project, an award-winning project that helped
  kids get to know and appreciate their grandparents' experiences.
Title Page: Children from around the world share food and customs
  from their cultures at a Children's International Summer Village.

Library and Archives Canada Cataloguing in Publication

Aloian, Molly
  Live it: respect / Molly Aloian.

(Crabtree character sketches)
Includes index.
ISBN 978-0-7787-4879-3 (bound).--ISBN 978-0-7787-4912-7 (pbk.)

  1. Respect--Juvenile literature. 2. Biography--Juvenile literature.
I. Title. II. Title: Respect. III. Series: Crabtree character sketches

BJ1533.R4A46 2010

j179.9   C2009-904985-6

Library of Congress Cataloging-in-Publication Data

Aloian, Molly.
  Live it : respect / Molly Aloian.
    p. cm. -- (Crabtree character sketches)
  Includes index.
  ISBN 978-0-7787-4912-7 (pbk. : alk. paper) -- ISBN 978-0-7787-4879-3
(reinforced library binding : alk. paper)
  1. Respect--Juvenile literature. 2. Biography--Juvenile literature. I.
Title.

  BJ1533.R4A56 2009
  179'.9--dc22
                              2009033253

Crabtree Publishing Company

www.crabtreebooks.com   1-800-387-7650

Printed in the USA/122009/BG20090930

Published in Canada
Crabtree Publishing
616 Welland Ave.
St. Catharines, ON
L2M 5V6

Published in the United States
Crabtree Publishing
PMB 59051
350 Fifth Avenue, 59th Floor
New York, New York 10118

Published in the United Kingdom
Crabtree Publishing
Maritime House
Basin Road North, Hove
BN41 1WR

Published in Australia
Crabtree Publishing
386 Mt. Alexander Rd.
Ascot Vale (Melbourne)
VIC 3032

CONTENTS

WHAT IS RESPECT? 4

RESPECTING TRADITIONS
AND HERITAGE 6

RESPECTING
THE ENVIRONMENT 10

RESPECTING
DIFFERENT CULTURES 14

RESPECTING WOMEN 18

RESPECTING
YOUR FAMILY 22

RESPECTING
WORKING PEOPLE 26

WEB SITES 30

GLOSSARY 31

INDEX 32

WHAT IS RESPECT?

RESPECT IS A VALUE— SOMETHING THAT'S IMPORTANT TO LIVING A GOOD LIFE.

RESPECT MEANS CONSIDERING THE RIGHTS, NEEDS, AND FEELINGS OF PEOPLE, ANIMALS, AND THE ENVIRONMENT.

THE PEOPLE YOU WILL READ ABOUT IN THIS BOOK SHOW RESPECT IN DIFFERENT SITUATIONS AND FOR DIFFERENT REASONS. READ THEIR STORIES TO LEARN MORE ABOUT HOW THESE REMARKABLE PEOPLE SHOWED RESPECT THROUGH THEIR ACTIONS.

SANDY KOUFAX
NATIONAL LEAGUE PITCHER FOR THE BROOKLYN/LOS ANGELES DODGERS

DAVID SUZUKI
AWARD-WINNING SCIENTIST, AUTHOR, *ENVIRONMENTALIST*, AND BROADCASTER

DR. DORIS ALLEN
FOUNDER OF CISV INTERNATIONAL

ELIZABETH CADY STANTON
WOMEN'S RIGHTS ACTIVIST

WILLIAM LLOYD GARRISON
ABOLITIONIST

STUDENTS, TEACHERS, PARENTS, AND
GRANDPARENTS INVOLVED IN
"THE GRANDPARENT PROJECT"

LEONARD ABESS JR.
BANKER

SANDY KOUFAX

WHO IS HE?
FORMER PITCHER FOR THE BROOKLYN/LOS ANGELES DODGERS

WHY HIM?
IN 1965, HE REFUSED TO PITCH IN GAME 1 OF THE WORLD SERIES BECAUSE THE GAME WAS ON THE SAME DAY AS AN IMPORTANT JEWISH HOLIDAY.

SANDY KOUFAX WAS AN OUTSTANDING PITCHER. HE LOVED PLAYING BASEBALL, BUT HE ALSO RESPECTED THE **TRADITIONS** OF HIS JEWISH HERITAGE. LET'S SEE HOW HE SHOWED THAT RESPECT.

IT'S 1964. SANDY KOUFAX IS PITCHING AGAINST THE CINCINNATI REDS.

JUST ONE MORE...

YOU'RE OUT!

WOW! KOUFAX JUST PITCHED HIS THIRD NO-HITTER! HE'S GOTTA BE THE BEST PITCHER IN THE LEAGUE!

I CAN'T PITCH IN GAME 1, BOYS. IT'S ON THE SAME DAY AS YOM KIPPUR.

YOU HAVE TO PLAY, SANDY! WE NEED YOU!

WE CAN'T WIN WITHOUT YOU!

SOME THINGS ARE MORE IMPORTANT THAN BASEBALL.

KOUFAX'S DECISION SHOCKED AND SURPRISED THE COUNTRY. SOME PEOPLE PRAISED HIM. MANY CRITICIZED HIM AND SAID HE HAD LET HIS TEAM DOWN.

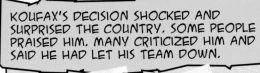

PLAY OR PRAY?

FOLKS, I DON'T KNOW ABOUT YOU, BUT TO ME, WHAT KOUFAX IS DOING IS JUST PLAIN UNPROFESSIONAL.

RESPECTING THE ENVIRONMENT

DAVID SUZUKI

DAVID SUZUKI'S BOOKS AND TV SHOWS HAVE INSPIRED MILLIONS OF VIEWERS IN OVER **50** COUNTRIES AROUND THE WORLD.

THINK OF THE CARS WE DRIVE EVERY DAY, THEIR ENVIRONMENTAL COST, THE PROBLEMS OF **SUSTAINABILITY**, AND **CONGESTED** ROADS. CARS ARE LOOKING A LOT MORE LIKE PROBLEMS THAN PLAYTHINGS! *

BUT MAYBE THIS WILL GET PEOPLE HEADED IN THE RIGHT DIRECTION!

WHO IS HE?
AN AWARD-WINNING SCIENTIST, AUTHOR, ENVIRONMENTALIST, AND BROADCASTER

WHY HIM?
IN 1990, HE CREATED THE DAVID SUZUKI NATURE CHALLENGE TO TEACH OTHERS HOW TO SHOW RESPECT FOR THE ENVIRONMENT.

HOW OFTEN DO YOU THINK ABOUT YOUR IMPACT ON THE ENVIRONMENT? DAVID SUZUKI THINKS ABOUT IT EVERY DAY.

DR. SUZUKI WORKS TIRELESSLY TO FIND WAYS FOR PEOPLE TO LIVE IN BALANCE WITH THE NATURAL WORLD. KEEP READING TO FIND OUT HOW HE INSPIRED OTHERS TO RESPECT THE ENVIRONMENT AS MUCH AS HE DOES.

*ACTUAL QUOTE

PEOPLE FROM ALL OVER BEGAN TAKING THE NATURE CHALLENGE. SOME FAMILIES SWITCHED TO *HYBRID* CARS, WHICH RUN ON BOTH ELECTRICITY AND GAS.

OTHERS CHANGED WHERE THEY GOT THEIR FOOD.

THIS FARMER GREW THESE FRUITS AND VEGETABLES HIMSELF. BUYING LOCAL PRODUCE IS PART OF DAVID SUZUKI'S NATURE CHALLENGE.

MANY OTHER PEOPLE MADE LITTLE CHANGES AROUND THE HOUSE.

DAVID SUZUKI SAYS WE SHOULD USE COMPACT FLUORESCENT LIGHT BULBS. THEY'RE *75 PERCENT* MORE *EFFICIENT* THAN REGULAR LIGHT BULBS.

NATURE TAKES CARE OF US. NATURE CLEANS OUR AIR AND WATER, MAKES THE SOIL THAT GROWS OUR FOOD, AND PROVIDES THE **RESOURCES** TO MAKE ALL OUR MATERIAL GOODS. NATURE IS OUR HOME. AND JUST AS WE TAKE CARE OF OUR HOUSE, WE ALSO MUST TAKE CARE OF NATURE. *

DAVID SUZUKI HAS HELPED HUNDREDS OF THOUSANDS OF PEOPLE MAKE INDIVIDUAL CHOICES THAT RESPECT THE ENVIRONMENT. ARE YOU UP TO HIS CHALLENGE?

WHAT WOULD YOU DO?

TAKE A LOOK AT THESE TEN IDEAS FROM DAVID SUZUKI'S NATURE CHALLENGE FOR KIDS. WHICH ONES WILL YOU DO?

1. START TURNING THINGS OFF!
2. SPEND MORE TIME OUTSIDE. YOU'LL SAVE ELECTRICITY.
3. CHECK FOR HEAT LOSS IN YOUR HOME.
4. EAT MEAT-FREE MEALS ONE DAY A WEEK.
5. BUY LOCALLY GROWN AND PRODUCED FOOD.
6. SEE IF YOUR FAMILY CAR IS FUEL-EFFICIENT.
7. WALK, BIKE, OR TAKE A BUS.
8. FIND WAYS TO GET TO YOUR FAVORITE PLACES WITHOUT A CAR.
9. EXPRESS YOUR FEELINGS ABOUT NATURE IN ART.
10. ENCOURAGE FRIENDS TO TAKE THE NATURE CHALLENGE.

*ACTUAL QUOTE

RESPECTING DIFFERENT CULTURES

DR. DORIS ALLEN

WHO IS SHE?
FOUNDER OF CISV (CHILDREN'S INTERNATIONAL SUMMER VILLAGES). IN 1979, SHE WAS NOMINATED FOR THE NOBEL PEACE PRIZE.

WHY HER?
SHE BROUGHT TOGETHER CHILDREN FROM DIFFERENT NATIONS AND ENCOURAGED THEM TO LEARN ABOUT AND RESPECT EACH OTHER.

AFTER THE HORRORS OF WORLD WAR II, PEOPLE AROUND THE WORLD WERE THINKING OF WAYS TO CREATE A LASTING PEACE. FOR DR. DORIS ALLEN, THIS QUESTION WAS ESPECIALLY IMPORTANT.

THERE WON'T BE ANY MORE WARS, WILL THERE, MOM?

WELL, WE DON'T WANT THERE TO BE. SO I GUESS WE'LL HAVE TO DO EVERYTHING WE CAN TO STOP ANOTHER ONE FROM HAPPENING.

BUT WHAT CAN WE DO?

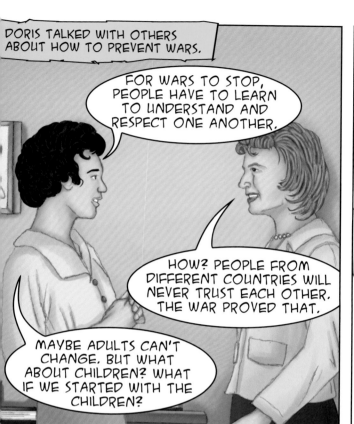

DORIS TALKED WITH OTHERS ABOUT HOW TO PREVENT WARS.

FOR WARS TO STOP, PEOPLE HAVE TO LEARN TO UNDERSTAND AND RESPECT ONE ANOTHER.

HOW? PEOPLE FROM DIFFERENT COUNTRIES WILL NEVER TRUST EACH OTHER. THE WAR PROVED THAT.

MAYBE ADULTS CAN'T CHANGE. BUT WHAT ABOUT CHILDREN? WHAT IF WE STARTED WITH THE CHILDREN?

WE COULD BRING TOGETHER CHILDREN FROM ALL OVER THE GLOBE. IT COULD BE LIKE A CAMP, OR VILLAGE! THEY'D LEARN TO LIKE AND RESPECT EACH OTHER WHILE THEY WERE HAVING FUN.

THEN PERHAPS THEY WON'T GO TO WAR WITH EACH OTHER WHEN THEY GROW UP.

CT TOOK DR. ALLEN FIVE YEARS TO ACCOMPLISH HER DREAM. BUT IN 1951, IN GLENDALE, OHIO...

WELCOME TO THE FIRST EVER CHILDREN'S INTERNATIONAL SUMMER VILLAGE! THERE ARE 60 OF YOU HERE, IN *DELEGATIONS* FROM EIGHT DIFFERENT COUNTRIES.

I'M SO EXCITED! WHERE ARE YOU FROM?

I'M FROM GERMANY.

IT'S HARD TO BELIEVE OUR COUNTRIES WERE AT WAR JUST A FEW YEARS AGO.

EVERY DAY, THE DELEGATES TOOK PART IN ACTIVITIES THAT HELPED THEM GET TO KNOW EACH OTHER. THEY ATE TOGETHER...

WHAT IS THIS STUFF?

IT'S WIENERSCHNITZEL, EVERYONE LOVES IT IN GERMANY!

THEY PLAYED TOGETHER,

THEY HAD SPECIAL FLAG CEREMONIES,

GUTEN TAG

GOOD MORNING

BONJOUR

BUENOS DIAS

AND THEY SANG SONGS,

HERE IN THIS VILLAGE YOU MAY SEE CHILDREN LIVING HAPPILY DIFFERENT *RACE* AND DIFFERENT LAND HERE WE COME TO UNDERSTAND ONE ANOTHER'S POINT OF VIEW LEARNING THROUGH THE THINGS WE DO HOW ALIKE AM I TO YOU. ✽

✽ ACTUAL QUOT

EACH DELEGATION SPONSORED A NATIONAL NIGHT TO TEACH THEIR FRIENDS ABOUT THEIR COUNTRY AND *CUSTOMS.*

SO THIS IS CALLED A TORTILLA?

I LOVE YOUR COSTUME! CAN YOU SHOW ME HOW TO DO THAT DANCE?

RESPECTING OTHER CULTURES MEANS TAKING THE TIME TO LEARN ABOUT THEM. I THINK WE'VE ALL DONE THAT.

I KNOW THAT MY LIFE HAS BEEN CHANGED FOREVER. *

I HOPE WE CAN HAVE THESE VILLAGES EVERY YEAR. AND I HOPE THAT THE CHILDREN AND YOUTH OF CISV WILL CONTINUE TO LEAD US TOWARD A MORE PEACEFUL WORLD.

SINCE 1951, NEARLY 200,000 PEOPLE FROM OVER 60 COUNTRIES HAVE PARTICIPATED IN CISV ACTIVITIES, BUT YOU DON'T HAVE TO GO TO ONE OF THEIR PROGRAMS TO SHOW RESPECT FOR OTHER CULTURES.

WHAT WOULD YOU DO?

IMAGINE YOU AND YOUR FRIENDS ARE JUST LEAVING SCHOOL FOR THE DAY. YOU WALK BY TWO OTHER KIDS WHO ARE DRESSED DIFFERENTLY AND SPEAKING A LANGUAGE YOU'RE NOT FAMILIAR WITH. WHAT COULD YOU SAY OR DO THAT WOULD SHOW THEM THAT YOU ARE INTERESTED IN THEM AND THEIR CULTURE?

*ACTUAL QUOTE

17

RESPECTING WOMEN

WILLIAM LLOYD GARRISON

ELIZABETH CADY STANTON

WHO ARE THEY?
WILLIAM LLOYD GARRISON WAS AN ABOLITIONIST AND A SUPPORTER OF THE WOMEN'S SUFFRAGE MOVEMENT. ELIZABETH CADY STANTON WAS ALSO AN ABOLITIONIST AND PLAYED AN IMPORTANT ROLE IN THE EARLY WOMEN'S RIGHTS MOVEMENT.

WHY THEM?
IN 1840, AT THE WORLD ANTI-SLAVERY CONVENTION IN LONDON, ENGLAND, WILLIAM LLOYD GARRISON AND ELIZABETH CADY STANTON BOTH STOOD UP FOR THEIR BELIEF THAT EVERY PERSON, REGARDLESS OF GENDER, DESERVED RESPECT FROM OTHERS.

ELIZABETH CADY STANTON AND HER HUSBAND, HENRY, ATTENDED THE WORLD ANTI-SLAVERY CONVENTION IN LONDON, JUST TWO DAYS AFTER THEY WERE MARRIED.

UNTIL THE EARLY 1900S, WOMEN HAD FAR FEWER RIGHTS THAN MEN. THEY WEREN'T ALLOWED TO VOTE OR OWN ANY PROPERTY. THEY WERE NOT CONSIDERED EQUAL TO MEN. READ ON TO FIND OUT HOW TWO PEOPLE SHOWED THAT WOMEN DESERVED RESPECT.

SHORTLY AFTER ARRIVING AT THE CONVENTION, ELIZABETH AND THE OTHER WOMEN WHO ATTENDED GOT AN UNWELCOME SURPRISE.

SHOULD WOMEN BE ALLOWED TO PARTICIPATE IN THIS CONVENTION? LET'S TAKE A VOTE!

WE AREN'T GOING TO BE ALLOWED TO TAKE PART IN THE CONVENTION EVEN THOUGH WE'VE BEEN ELECTED AS DELEGATES JUST LIKE THE MEN HAVE!

THESE MEN ARE NOT TREATING US FAIRLY!

I CAN MAKE A SPEECH ASKING FOR WOMEN TO BE INCLUDED IN THE CONVENTION, BUT I'M NOT SURE HOW MUCH GOOD IT WILL DO.

WE'VE VOTED, AND WOMEN ARE NOT ALLOWED TO SPEAK OR VOTE AT THIS CONVENTION! THE WOMEN MUST SIT SEPARATELY BEHIND THAT CURTAIN.

THAT JUST ISN'T FAIR!

ELIZABETH MET ANOTHER ABOLITIONIST NAMED LUCRETIA MOTT. THEY QUICKLY BECAME FRIENDS.

PLEASED TO MEET YOU, LUCRETIA.

AND YOU, ELIZABETH. I GUESS WE'LL BE SITTING TOGETHER TODAY.

THE EXPERIENCE AT THE CONVENTION MADE ELIZABETH CADY STANTON AND LUCRETIA MOTT EVEN MORE PASSIONATE ABOUT RIGHTS FOR WOMEN. IN 1848, ELIZABETH AND LUCRETIA WROTE A DOCUMENT CALLED THE DECLARATION OF RIGHTS AND SENTIMENTS. WILLIAM LLOYD GARRISON WAS ONE OF THE FIRST TO SIGN IT.

THE HISTORY OF THE PAST IS BUT ONE LONG STRUGGLE UPWARD TO *EQUALITY.* *

*ACTUAL QUOTE

WILLIAM LLOYD GARRISON SHOWED HIS RESPECT FOR WOMEN BY PROTESTING HOW THEY HAD BEEN TREATED. HE CAUSED OTHER PEOPLE TO RETHINK THEIR ATTITUDE, TOO.

WHAT WOULD YOU DO?

PICTURE YOURSELF IN THIS SITUATION: YOU'RE ON A CO-ED HOCKEY TEAM. THE COACH LOVES TO WIN AND THINKS THE BOYS ARE STRONGER PLAYERS. IN MANY GAMES, THE BOYS GET MOST OF THE PLAYING TIME, AND THE GIRLS ARE LEFT SITTING ON THE BENCH. HOW COULD YOU CONVINCE THE COACH THAT ALL PLAYERS SHOULD HAVE AN OPPORTUNITY TO PLAY?

RESPECTING YOUR FAMILY

THE GRANDPARENT PROJECT

WHO ARE THEY?
A GROUP OF STUDENTS IN DENMARK WHO BECAME KNOWN FOR THEIR WORK ON THE GRANDPARENT PROJECT.

WHY THEM?
FOR FOUR YEARS, STUDENTS PARTICIPATED IN A SPECIAL PROJECT THAT TAUGHT THEM TO RESPECT AND **APPRECIATE** THE OLDER MEMBERS OF THEIR FAMILIES.

WHAT DO YOU KNOW ABOUT YOUR GRANDPARENTS? DO YOU KNOW AS MUCH AS YOU SHOULD? READ TO SEE HOW THESE STUDENTS LEARNED WHY THEY SHOULD **ADMIRE** AND RESPECT THEIR GRANDPARENTS.

WHEN THE GRANDPARENT PROJECT WAS FIRST INTRODUCED, NOT EVERY STUDENT WAS THRILLED...

THE GRANDPARENT PROJECT

$7 + 1 = 9$

THIS PROJECT WILL HELP YOU REALLY GET TO KNOW YOUR GRANDPARENTS!

OH, MAN! MY GRANDPARENTS ARE SO DULL!

THIS IS GONNA BE AWFUL.

FIRST, THE STUDENTS HAD TO THINK ABOUT ALL OF THE THINGS THEY WANTED TO LEARN ABOUT THEIR GRANDPARENTS.

SO, WHAT QUESTIONS ARE YOU GOING TO ASK ON YOUR **QUESTIONNAIRE?**

I'M GOING TO ASK WHAT KINDS OF TOYS MY GRANDFATHER PLAYED WITH WHEN HE WAS YOUNG.

THE STUDENTS LISTENED TO THEIR GRANDPARENTS' CHILDHOOD MEMORIES AND WROTE THEM DOWN.

AND THEN WHAT HAPPENED?!

THEY READ THE STORIES OUT LOUD OR MADE THEM INTO COMIC STRIPS!

AND IN THIS PANEL, HE'S HELPING HIS NEIGHBOR...

THE CHILDREN WERE AMAZED TO LEARN HOW INTERESTING THEIR GRANDPARENTS' LIVES WERE. THEY ALSO HAD FUN COMPARING THEIR OWN LIVES TO THAT OF THEIR GRANDPARENTS AT THAT AGE.

PARENTS GOT INVOLVED, TOO!

DAD, GRANDMA TOLD ME ABOUT WHEN YOU LIVED OVER THE GROCERY STORE. WHAT CAN YOU REMEMBER FROM THAT TIME?

THE STUDENTS WERE VERY PROUD OF THEIR GRANDPARENT PROJECT. IT TAUGHT THEM TO RESPECT THEIR PARENTS AND GRANDPARENTS.

TELLING YOU MY STORIES WAS FUN. THANK YOU FOR LISTENING.

MAYBE YOU CAN TELL ME SOME MORE WHEN YOU COME TO DINNER.

MY PARENTS AND GRANDPARENTS HAVE SOME REALLY COOL STORIES. I'M GLAD I GOT TO HEAR THEM.

ME, TOO.

Berliner Independe

LOCAL STUDENTS WIN GLOBAL JUNIOR CHALLENGE COMPETITION

FOR THEIR WORK ON THE GRANDPARENT PROJECT, THE STUDENTS WERE AWARDED A SPECIAL PRIZE AT THE FIRST ANNUAL GLOBAL JUNIOR CHALLENGE COMPETITION IN ROME, ITALY!

BUT THE BEST AWARD MAY HAVE BEEN WHAT THEY GAINED FROM LEARNING TO RESPECT THE LIVES AND EXPERIENCES OF THEIR GRANDPARENTS.

WHAT WOULD YOU DO?

THE NEXT TIME YOU VISIT YOUR GRANDPARENTS (OR ANYONE WHO'S OLDER), HOW COULD YOU SHOW THAT YOU RESPECT THEM? HERE'S ONE POSSIBILITY. THINK OF SIX QUESTIONS YOU COULD ASK ABOUT THEIR LIVES. TRY TO MAKE THE QUESTIONS FUN AND LISTEN CAREFULLY TO THE ANSWERS.

NOW, THINK OF TWO MORE WAYS YOU CAN SHOW RESPECT TO YOUR GRANDPARENTS...

RESPECTING WORKING PEOPLE

LEONARD ABESS JR.

WHO IS HE?
THE FORMER *CEO* OF NATIONAL CITY BANK IN MIAMI, FLORIDA

WHY HIM?
HE SHOWED HIS RESPECT FOR THE EMPLOYEES AT HIS BANK WITH AN AMAZING ACT OF GENEROSITY.

IT'S IMPORTANT TO RESPECT THE PEOPLE WHO WORK HARD AT THEIR JOBS, FROM SALES CLERKS TO FOOD SERVERS TO *SANITATION* WORKERS. LEONARD ABESS JR. KNOWS THAT. LET'S SEE WHAT HE DID TO SHOW HIS OWN WORKERS HOW MUCH HE APPRECIATED THEM.

LEONARD ABESS JR. STARTED HIS CAREER IN THE PRINT SHOP AT HIS FATHER'S BANK.

HOW ARE YOU DOING, SON?

OKAY, DAD. BUT THIS IS HARDER THAN I THOUGHT IT WOULD BE!

AS HE SLOWLY WORKED HIS WAY UP IN THE BANK, LEONARD REALIZED THE IMPORTANCE OF ALL THE EMPLOYEES.

DEPOSITS

IF THE PRESIDENT DOESN'T COME TO WORK IT'S NOT A BIG DEAL. BUT IF THE TELLERS DON'T SHOW UP, IT'S A BIG PROBLEM. *

*ACTUAL QUOT

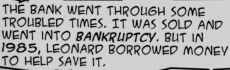

THE BANK WENT THROUGH SOME TROUBLED TIMES. IT WAS SOLD AND WENT INTO *BANKRUPTCY.* BUT IN 1985, LEONARD BORROWED MONEY TO HELP SAVE IT.

GOOD LUCK, MR. ABESS. YOU'RE GOING TO NEED IT.

UNDER LEONARD'S OWNERSHIP, THE BANK GREW FROM $400 MILLION IN *ASSETS* TO OVER $2.5 BILLION.

Annual Employee Dinner

IT'S BEEN ANOTHER GREAT YEAR, MR. ABESS. CONGRATULATIONS!

DON'T CONGRATULATE ME. WE'VE DONE WELL THANKS TO ALL OF YOU!

BUT THEN IT WAS TIME FOR A CHANGE.

SO YOU'RE REALLY GOING TO SELL THE BANK?

YES, IT'S TIME. AND I'VE GOTTEN A GREAT OFFER. I'M JUST A LITTLE WORRIED ABOUT THE PEOPLE WHO WORK THERE. I'VE KNOWN SOME OF THEM SINCE I WAS SEVEN YEARS OLD!

BUT LEONARD FIGURED OUT WHAT TO DO.

ARE YOU SURE, MR. ABESS? THIS IS 60 MILLION DOLLARS!! AND BY RIGHTS IT BELONGS TO YOU!

I HAVE MORE THAN ENOUGH MONEY; AND MY EMPLOYEES DESERVE IT FOR ALL THE YEARS THEY SUPPORTED ME. IN A WAY, THIS IS THEIR MONEY, TOO.

27

LEONARD DIDN'T WANT ANY *PUBLICITY* FOR WHAT HE DID. BUT HIS EMPLOYEES MADE SURE PEOPLE FOUND OUT.

I ALWAYS PLANNED TO DO SOMETHING LIKE THIS SOMEDAY. I JUST WONDER IF I DID ENOUGH.

[E]VEN PRESIDENT BARACK OBAMA LEARNED [W]HAT ABESS HAD DONE AND *HAILED* HIM [A]S A NATIONAL *INSPIRATION.*

IN MY LIFE, I HAVE ALSO LEARNED THAT HOPE IS FOUND IN UNLIKELY PLACES...

I THINK ABOUT LEONARD ABESS, ... WHO TOOK A *$60* MILLION BONUS AND GAVE IT OUT TO ALL *399* PEOPLE WHO WORKED FOR HIM. *

LEONARD ABESS JR. SHOWED WHAT IT MEANS TO RESPECT EVERY WORKER, NOT JUST THE ONES WHO HAVE IMPORTANT TITLES OR MAKE A LOT OF MONEY.

WHAT WOULD YOU DO?

YOUR SCHOOL HAS A CARNIVAL TWICE A YEAR. IT'S ALWAYS FUN: THERE'S A DJ AND GAMES AND PLENTY OF SNACKS. THIS YEAR, THOUGH, SOME OF YOUR FRIENDS START PULLING DOWN THE STREAMERS AND POPPING THE BALLOONS.

"YOU'RE TRASHING THE PLACE!" YOU SAY.

"SO WHAT?" THEY REPLY. "THE JANITOR WILL CLEAN IT UP."

WHAT WOULD YOU SAY?

* ACTUAL QUOTE

29

WEB SITES

LEARN MORE ABOUT DAVID SUZUKI'S NATURE CHALLENGE AND HOW YOU CAN RESPECT THE ENVIRONMENT EACH DAY.

www.davidsuzuki.org/NatureChallenge/Default.asp

THE CHILDREN'S INTERNATIONAL SUMMER VILLAGE SITE WILL TELL YOU MORE ABOUT THE GROUP'S HISTORY AND WHAT IT'S DOING TODAY.

www.cisv.org/

THIS TIMELINE OF THE WOMEN'S RIGHTS MOVEMENT WILL TEACH YOU MORE ABOUT WOMEN'S FIGHT FOR RESPECT.

www.ibiblio.org/prism/mar98/path.html

FOR ACTUAL MATERIAL FROM THE GRANDPARENT PROJECT, VISIT THE AMAZING KIDS SITE.

www.amazing-kids.org/kids5-01.htm

THIS SITE WILL GUIDE YOU THROUGH THE DEFINITIONS OF RESPECT AND TELL YOU HOW TO COMMUNICATE RESPECTFULLY.

www.itsnotok.org/whatisrespect.html

GLOSSARY

ABOLITIONIST A PERSON WHO BELIEVED IN AND WORKED TOWARD AN END TO SLAVERY

ADMIRE TO HAVE HIGH REGARD FOR

APPRECIATE TO BE GRATEFUL FOR SOMETHING

ASSETS PROPERTY THAT IS CONSIDERED TO HAVE VALUE; COULD BE USED TO PAY OFF DEBTS

BANKRUPTCY THE CONDITION OF BEING BANKRUPT, OR UNABLE TO PAY DEBTS

CEO CHIEF EXECUTIVE OFFICER, THE PERSON WHO MAKES DECISIONS FOR A BUSINESS

CONGESTED BLOCKED OR TOO FULL

CONVENTION A LARGE MEETING OR CONFERENCE

CUSTOMS THE USUAL WAY A PERSON OR GROUP DOES THINGS

DELEGATIONS A GROUP CHOSEN TO REPRESENT OTHERS

EFFICIENT ABLE TO PRODUCE RESULTS WITHOUT WASTE

ENVIRONMENTALIST A PERSON WHO IS CONCERNED ABOUT THE ENVIRONMENT

EQUALITY THE STATE OF BEING EQUAL

GENDER THE STATE OF BEING MALE OR FEMALE

HAILED CALLED; RECOGNIZED AS

HYBRID SOMETHING FORMED BY COMBINING PARTS OF OTHER THINGS

INSPIRATION SOMEONE OR SOMETHING THAT MAKES A PERSON FEEL OR WANT TO DO SOMETHING

PUBLICITY ATTENTION GIVEN TO SOMEONE BY THE MEDIA

QUESTIONNAIRE A SET OF QUESTIONS, USUALLY DESIGNED TO GATHER INFORMATION

RACE A GROUP OF PEOPLE OF COMMON ANCESTRY

RESOURCES THINGS PEOPLE NEED

SANITATION THE MEANS OF KEEPING THINGS CLEAN AND HEALTHY

SUFFRAGE THE RIGHT TO VOTE

SUSTAINABILITY THE ABILITY TO SUPPORT OR SUSTAIN SOMETHING

SYNAGOGUE A PLACE WHERE JEWISH PEOPLE WORSHIP

TRADITIONS BELIEFS OR CUSTOMS

INDEX

ABESS JR., LEONARD 5, 26, 27, 28, 29

ABOLITIONIST 5, 18, 19

ALLEN, DORIS 5, 14, 15, 16, 17

ANTI-SLAVERY CONVENTION 18

ASSETS 27

BANKRUPTCY 27

BASEBALL 6, 7, 8

CHILDREN'S INTERNATIONAL SUMMER VILLAGES (CISV) 5, 14, 15, 17

DECLARATION OF RIGHTS AND SENTIMENTS 21

DELEGATION 15, 16, 17, 19

DENMARK 22

ENVIRONMENTALIST 4, 10

EQUALITY 21

FLORIDA, USA 26

GARRISON, WILLIAM LLOYD 5, 18, 20, 21

GENDER 18

GENEROSITY 26

GLENDALE, OHIO, USA 15

GRANDPARENT PROJECT, THE 5, 22, 23, 24, 25

HERITAGE 6

HYBRID CARS 12

INSPIRATION 29

KOUFAX, SANDY 4, 6, 7, 8, 9

MEMORIES 24

NOBEL PEACE PRIZE 14

OBAMA, BARACK 29

RACE 16

RESOURCES 13

RIGHTS 4, 5, 18, 21, 27

ROME, ITALY 25

STANTON, ELIZABETH CADY 5, 18, 19, 21

SUSTAINABILITY 10

SUZUKI, DAVID 4, 10, 11, 12, 13

SYNAGOGUE 9

WIENERSCHNITZEL 16

WOMEN'S SUFFRAGE MOVEMENT 18

YOM KIPPUR 7, 8